This Book Belongs To

____

Made in the USA
Columbia, SC
24 November 2019

83763553R00061